Publisher's Preface

Robert Gallagher
Publisher
Saint Benedict Press, LLC
TAN Books

Has God placed this booklet in your hands? Is He giving you an introduction to the weapons and strategies of spiritual warfare? This little guide will be a trusted field manual to help you navigate Dom Lorenzo Scupoli's famous treatise on conquering sin through spiritual combat in order to obtain peace in your soul.

The Classics Made Simple series aims to introduce the great works of Catholic literature to a wide readership. The Classics of the Faith are not meant only for saints and scholars: they're meant for everyone. They're wise, human, practical, and they have something important to say to each of us.

The Classics are also timeless. Other books come and go, passing with the tastes and fads of each generation. But the Catholic Classics remain and God has used them to teach and sanctify men and women of every age.

We hope this *TAN Guide* will stir within you a desire to read *The Spiritual Combat*, or if you've already read it, to re-read it with a renewed interest. You'll discover each *TAN Guide* is a perfect vehicle to introduce your newest favorite Classic to your friends and family. Give this little booklet a few minutes of your time and see what happens!

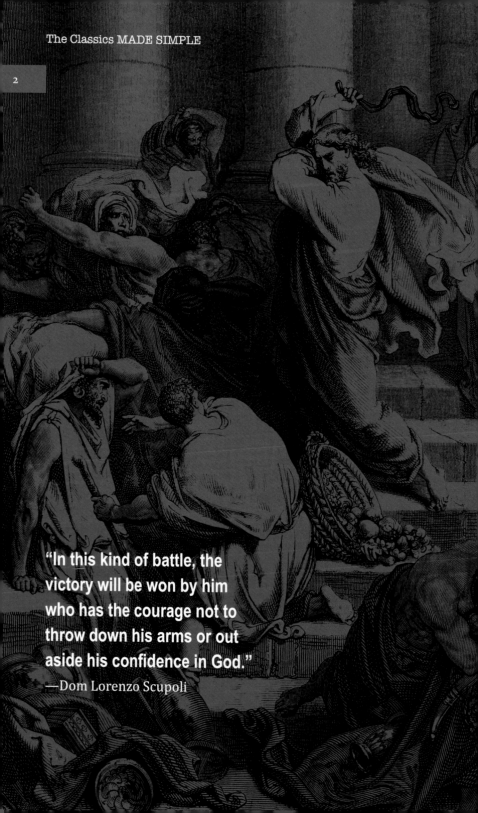

"In this kind of battle, the victory will be won by him who has the courage not to throw down his arms or out aside his confidence in God."
—Dom Lorenzo Scupoli

Introduction to—*The Spiritual Combat*

Imagine a book whose insights are so valuable that you carry a copy with you everywhere for years and read from it every day. To the sixteenth-century bishop and Church Doctor St. Francis de Sales, that book was *The Spiritual Combat*, which he carried in his pocket for eighteen years, reading from it daily and recommending it to all those in his spiritual care.

Written by Dom Lorenzo Scupoli of the Theatine Order, *The Spiritual Combat* is meant to guide us on the path to eternal life and happiness, which come through spiritual perfection. This perfection consists, not in outward practices, but in knowing and loving God and in mastering our vices, so that we may submit ourselves completely to God's will out of a desire to please Him. We reach this perfection through a constant struggle against our fallen nature, which tends to lure us away from our goal. Dom Scupoli's words are urgent:

"You must wage continual warfare against yourself and employ your entire strength in demolishing each vicious inclination, however trivial. Consequently, in preparing for the combat you must summon up all your resolution and courage. No one shall be rewarded with a crown who has not fought courageously."

We cannot simply walk away from this struggle. "This war is unavoidable," Dom Scupoli tells us, "and you must either fight or die." But how are we to fight? *The Spiritual Combat* provides us with a battle plan for all we need to do so: the weapons we must use; what we can expect as we progress in the spiritual life; how we must prepare for and face battles; how we must bear defeats; and how we can face with confidence the ultimate battle at the moment of our death. Let's look at the weapons we need for our spiritual combat and how we can acquire them.

First Weapon: Distrust of Ourselves
The first spiritual weapon is *distrust of ourselves*—that is, the realization that we are weak and that our fallen nature makes us liable to sin. Without this weapon, Dom Scupoli warns, we can't hope to overcome even our weakest passions. We must convince ourselves of its necessity, because we have a tendency to overestimate our abilities and our importance.

Although distrust of our strength is a gift of God, we have to work to obtain it, and Dom Scupoli gives us four ways to do so:

1. We must consider our powerlessness to do any good without God's help.

2. We must ask God, humbly and earnestly, to grant us the grace to distrust ourselves.

3. We must gradually accustom ourselves to distrust our strength and the illusions of our mind.

4. Whenever we do commit a fault, we must try to discover our vulnerabilities, knowing that God permits our failures so that we may develop greater knowledge of ourselves.

Second Weapon: Confidence in God

As we learn to distrust ourselves, we must place all our *confidence in God*, trusting that He who created us for eternal life with Him will provide us with all we need to attain that goal. Again Dom Scupoli recommends four ways to acquire this confidence:

1. We must humbly ask God to grant us confidence in Him.

2. We must think deeply about God's immense power, His infinite wisdom, His unlimited goodness, and His readiness to give all that is needed to those who love Him. Contemplating these attributes will help to convince us that God knows our needs and is able and willing to fulfill them.

Old Conflicts and a New World

1530
Lorenzo (Francesco) Scupoli born in Otranto, Italy.

1530

Ahmad ibn Ibrahim "the Conqueror" leads Muslim Somalis in a holy war against Christian Ethiopia, wreaking great damage on the kingdom and its churches and shrines.

1530

Charles V of Spain, king of Sicily, gives the Knights Hospitaller the Mediterranean archipelago country of Malta in exchange for an annual fee of a single Maltese falcon, which they send to a representative of the king on All Souls Day.

1531

Our Lady appears to an Aztec peasant on a hill near Mexico City. The Virgin of Guadalupe requests the construction of a church and imprints her image on Juan Diego's *tilma* as a sign.

3. We must recall the numerous scriptural examples and assurances of God's providing for those who trust in Him.

4. Finally, before performing a good action or considering a failure of ours, we should remind ourselves of our own weakness, on one hand, and God's infinite power, wisdom, and goodness on the other.

Knowing how easily we fool ourselves, Dom Scupoli offers a test to prove whether we have truly developed distrust of ourselves and confidence in God. If we have developed these weapons, our faults and failures will neither surprise us nor cause us despair. We will be sorry for them, of course, but we won't lose our peace of mind. We will simply attribute them to our own weakness and renew our hope and prayer for God's help.

Third Weapon: The Proper Use of Our Mind and Body

The third weapon in our spiritual arsenal is the *proper use of our mind* (that is, our understanding and our will) and *our body* toward spiritual perfection.

The first step, Dom Scupoli counsels, is to free our minds of ignorance and curiosity. To overcome ignorance, we must distinguish between what is good and what is evil, and between truth and falsehood, by diligently examining everything, not by appearances or according to our senses or by what the world thinks, but by the light of the Holy Spirit, for which we must pray. To rid our mind of curiosity, we must

1537

The first conservatories of music are founded in Naples and Venice. In orphanages attached to hospitals, the orphans (*conservati* in Italian) are given a musical education; the term "conservatory" came to apply to all music schools.

1541-1542

St. Francis Xavier, companion of St. Ignatius Loyola and the first missionary of the Counter-Reformation, sets sail from Lisbon and reaches Goa, India; thus beginning his great nine-year mission to the East.

1543

Flemish Andreas Vesalius, considered the founder of modern human anatomy, publishes *De humani corporis fabrica (On the Fabric of the Human Body).*

not let it wander aimlessly or become consumed with worldly things, gossip, or an overwhelming desire for news. A disciplined mind will help us to focus on Christ and on what He asks of us.

As well as regulating our mind, we must conform our will entirely to the will of God and must act always with a desire to please Him. Dom Scupoli cautions us here that we must be on guard against performing even good acts out of self-love or for the pleasure they bring us, rather than out of love for God. Before acting, we must first consider God and whether the action coincides with His will and whether we desire it because it pleases only Him. When we develop a habit of doing this, our will becomes more aligned with God's will.

Finally, we must regulate our senses so that they may assist us in our spiritual growth. Dom Scupoli offers numerous examples of how the many things that please our senses may lift our minds to contemplate God rather than luring us into worldliness.

Fourth Weapon: Prayer

The fourth weapon is prayer, which draws us closer to God and motivates and strengthens us in our spiritual combat. Dom Scupoli presents various elements that make prayer more effective, including a willingness to please God and serve Him for His own sake, rather than to please ourselves; an ardent faith in God's goodness and providence; gratitude for blessings received; an awareness that petitions are granted through Christ's merits; and persistence.

Old Conflicts and a New World

c. 1570
Scupoli joins the Theatines and makes his novitiate under St. Andrew Avellino.

1567

On Mary Queen of Scots's removal from the throne, her one-year-old son succeeds her as James VI. The young king grows up as a hostage in Stirling Castle until he escapes at the age of 14 and asserts his authority.

1569

Flemish cartographer Gerardus Mercator publishes a map of the world, using the projection now known by his name. He also devises a technique to mass-produce globes using papier-mâché and maps printed with curved edges.

1577

Domenikos Theotokopoulos moves to Spain, where he is given the nickname El Greco. Best known for dramatically elongated figures and intense and unusual pigmentation, the artist's style evokes puzzlement from his contemporaries but great appreciation centuries later.

In addition to numerous examples of prayers for various situations, *The Spiritual Combat* explains different *methods* of prayer. One is meditation, by which we ponder Christ's example of holiness in order to imitate it and improve ourselves. Another is asking the assistance, or intercession, of the angels and saints, particularly the Blessed Virgin Mary. To help us practice this exercise regularly, Dom Scupoli suggests that we pray to certain intercessors on fixed days: on Sundays, the angels; on Mondays, John the Baptist; on Tuesdays, the patriarchs and prophets; on Wednesdays, the Apostles; on Thursdays, the martyrs; on Fridays, bishops and confessors; on Saturdays, the virgins and other saints. But every day, he adds, we should ask the assistance of Our Lady, our guardian angel, the archangel St. Michael, and any other saints to whom we are devoted, and we should pray that St. Joseph may protect us.

Additional Defenses: The Sacraments

Aside from these four weapons to be used in the spiritual combat, Dom Scupoli recommends the Holy Eucharist as a means of overcoming our spiritual enemies. He offers numerous points and prayers to help us prepare to receive this Sacrament devoutly by stirring our heart to a greater love for God and a greater sorrow for our sins.

When we cannot receive the Eucharist sacramentally, we can make a spiritual communion—by fervently desiring to receive Jesus in the Blessed Sacrament and then lovingly embracing Him as if we had received Him. Spiritual

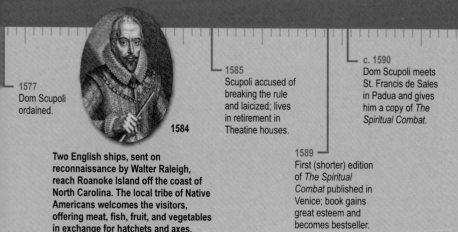

1577
Dom Scupoli ordained.

1584

Two English ships, sent on reconnaissance by Walter Raleigh, reach Roanoke Island off the coast of North Carolina. The local tribe of Native Americans welcomes the visitors, offering meat, fish, fruit, and vegetables in exchange for hatchets and axes.

1585
Scupoli accused of breaking the rule and laicized; lives in retirement in Theatine houses.

1589
First (shorter) edition of *The Spiritual Combat* published in Venice; book gains great esteem and becomes bestseller.

c. 1590
Dom Scupoli meets St. Francis de Sales in Padua and gives him a copy of *The Spiritual Combat*.

communion, as Bl. Pope John Paul II wrote, helps "cultivate in our hearts a constant desire for the Sacrament of the Eucharist." Dom Scupoli asserts, "Spiritual communion is sometimes of greater benefit to the soul and more acceptable to God than many sacramental Communions received with little preparation and less affection."

Finally, Dom Scupoli recommends that we seek forgiveness regularly through sacramental confession, through which we gain a greater awareness of our weaknesses, spiritual direction for overcoming them, and the grace to fight bravely in the spiritual combat.

Wielding Our Spiritual Weapons

With these spiritual weapons, our best defense against the injuries, insults, and disturbances that lead us into sin is to steel ourselves against them through foresight and preparation. With a keen understanding of human nature, Dom Scupoli cautions us against likely pitfalls, reminds us that we must not become prideful over our victories, and explains how the devil tries to lure us away from our goal.

As well prepared as we might be for battles, we are bound to be wounded now and then. At such times, Dom Scupoli assures us, we must not panic or lose heart, but must renew our confidence in God, remembering that He is able to help us grow in holiness through our humble acceptance of our failures.

Dom Scupoli shows understanding of the difficulties we face in our battles. He knows that we will have setbacks,

Old Conflicts and a New World

1597

Potato salad is mentioned in a book for the first time, describing how potatoes—a New World food introduced to Europe by Spanish explorers in the sixteenth century—are sometimes roasted and dressed in oil, vinegar, and salt according to individual tastes.

November 28, 1610
Scupoli dies; first edition of *The Spiritual Combat* bearing his name published.

1599

Jules Charles, a French botanist, builds the first practical modern greenhouse in Leiden, Holland, to grow medicinal tropical plants and citrus fruits.

1623

The Plymouth colonists celebrate their first "Thanksgiving"—not as a feast, but as a lengthy church servi affirming their gratitude to God. In preparation, the Separatists observ a Day of Humiliation, fasting and pr ing for reconciliation with God.

and he offers encouragement and motivation to continue in our efforts.

Replacing Vices with Virtues

As part of our spiritual combat, we must not only strive to conquer our vices; we must also seek to develop the opposite virtues. Those who are prone to sins of pride, for instance, should make frequent acts of humility. Dom Scupoli offers a systematic method for acquiring virtue: by developing only one virtue at a time and by degrees; by resolving each morning to strive to cultivate that virtue and by examining throughout the day our faithfulness to that resolution; by reflecting on the examples of the saints and meditating on Christ's life and death; by reading related inspirational passages from Scripture; and by practicing both exterior and interior acts of the virtue.

The Final Battle

The final chapters of *The Spiritual Combat* concern a proper preparation for death so that we may be ready for the most important battle of the spiritual life—whenever our time to face it might come. First, Dom Scupoli exhorts us to persevere in the spiritual combat throughout our life. He then offers methods and prayers to help us overcome fears and temptations we might face at the hour of death. Our persistence and readiness will help us face death, not with fear, but with confidence in God and a hopeful eagerness to see Him face-to-face.

With so much practical wisdom on how to achieve spiritual perfection, it's no wonder that *The Spiritual Combat* has remained a popular Classic after more than 400 years since its publication. If, like St. Francis de Sales, we take Dom Scupoli as our spiritual director, so to speak, and read just one brief chapter from his book each day, we will find wisdom to contemplate, prayers to say, and practical steps to help us daily grow closer to eternal happiness. ◆

◆

"Fight, therefore, with great determination. Do not let the weakness of your nature be an excuse. If your strength fails you, ask more from God. He will not refuse your request."

—Dom Lorenzo Scupoli

Conquer Your Own Will

An excerpt from *The Spiritual Combat*

Christian soul! If you seek to reach the loftiest peak of perfection, and to unite yourself so intimately with God that you become one in spirit with Him, you must first know the true nature and perfection of spirituality in order to succeed in the most sublime undertaking that can be expressed or imagined.

Some, who judge only by appearances, make it consist in penances, in hair shirts, austerities of the flesh, vigils, fasting, and similar bodily mortifications. Others, particularly women, fancy themselves extremely virtuous when they indulge in long vocal prayers, hear several Masses, spend many hours in church. . . . Others, and this does not exclude some of the religious who have consecrated themselves to God, think that perfection consists in perfect attendance in choir, in observing silence and retirement, and in a strict observance of their rule. Consequently, different people place perfection in different practices. It is certain that they all equally deceive themselves.

[The spiritual life] actually consists in knowing the infinite greatness and goodness of God, together with a true sense of our weakness and tendency to evil, in loving God and hating ourselves, in humbling ourselves not only before Him, but, for His sake, before all men, in renouncing entirely our own will in order to follow His. It consists, finally, in doing all of this solely for the glory of His Holy Name, for only one purpose—to please Him, for only one motive—that He should be loved and served by all His creatures.

These are the dictates of that law of love which the Holy Ghost has written on the hearts of the faithful. This is the way we must practice that self-denial so earnestly recommended by our Saviour in the Gospel. This it is that renders His yoke so sweet, His burden so light.

Since, therefore, you seek the highest degree of perfection, you must wage continual warfare against yourself and employ your entire strength in demolishing each vicious inclination, however trivial. Consequently, in preparing for the combat you must summon up all your resolution and courage.

For whoever has the courage to conquer his passions, to subdue his appetites, and repulse even the least motions of his own will, performs an action more meritorious in the sight of God than if, without this, he should tear his flesh with the sharpest disciplines, fast with greater austerity than the ancient Fathers of the Desert, or convert multitudes of sinners.

The conversion of a soul is, without doubt, infinitely more acceptable to the Divine Majesty than the mortification of a disorderly affection. Yet, every person, in his own particular sphere, should begin with what is immediately required of him. Now what God expects of us, above all else, is a serious application to conquering our passions; and this is more properly the accomplishment of our duty than if, with uncontrolled appetite, we should do Him a greater service. ◆

The Life of Dom Lorenzo Scupoli

Francesco Scupoli was born in Otranto, Italy, in 1530. Little is known about his early life until, at age thirty-nine, he joined the Theatines, a religious order dedicated to the cultivation of virtues, to teaching and preaching, and to caring for the sick and the imprisoned. He began his novitiate under the great spiritual director and preacher St. Andrew Avellino. After completing the preparation phase in 1571, he took the name Lorenzo. He was ordained in 1577 and worked in Milan and in Genoa, where he tended those afflicted by the Plague. Dom Scupoli observed the rule of his order strictly, prayed with diligence, and treasured solitude and silence.

He continued his ministry contentedly until 1585, when a humiliating ordeal began for him. By a ruling of his order, Dom Scupoli was imprisoned for a year, and then was reduced to the status of a lay brother and denied permission to exercise his priestly ministry. The cause for this harsh punishment—possibly a calumny—remains a mystery, because all the papers related to the trial were burned after the verdict was reconsidered a year later. In 1610, he was finally permitted to resume his priestly ministry, but he fell ill and died later that year.

Those twenty-five years spent in the school of suffering bore great fruit in Dom Scupoli's life and in the lives of others. Whatever he was accused of, he made no appeal, but accepted his censure as God's will. Because of his humble, resigned acceptance and the holiness with which he lived out his sentence, others regarded him as a man of great virtue.

But greater than the Christ-like example that he set for those around him was the Classic spiritual guide that he wrote during this time for readers

1530 —Born Francesco Scupoli in Otranto, Italy

1577 —Ordained a priest at the late age of forty-seven

1585 —Imprisoned and censured by his order; period of trials begins

1589 —First edition of *The Spiritual Combat* published in Venice

1610 —Priestly faculties restored, shortly before his death in the same year

of all times and places: *The Spiritual Combat,* which surely reflects the holy wisdom and enlightenment he gained through prayer and patient endurance. The humble prayers throughout the book, and the clear recognition that God permits our sufferings and struggles to help us grow holier, illustrate Dom Scupoli's strong faith in the tender love of God, even during this difficult time. Thus, both his life and his Classic work, *The Spiritual Combat,* reveal Dom Scupoli to be a sure guide on the path to spiritual perfection. ◆

◆

"Consider this—if the fury of your enemies is great, and their numbers overwhelming, the love which God holds for you is infinitely greater."

—Dom Lorenzo Scupoli

Biography

Notable Theatine Saints

Lorenzo Scupoli was a priest of the Theatine Order, also known as the Congregation of Clerks Regular of the Divine Providence, which was founded in 1524 by St. Cajetan, Paolo Consiglieri, Bonifacio da Colle, and Giovanni Pietro Carafa, Bishop of Theate (and later Pope Paul IV).

The order's mission was to the exhort the clergy, many of whom had grown lax, to a more zealous spiritual life, and to help laypersons cultivate virtue—an appeal that is reflected in *The Spiritual Combat.* The order's founding members fought diligently against the errors of Martin Luther and strove to keep them from spreading to Italy.

Despite their strict rule of life and vow of poverty, the congregation grew rapidly. The Theatines founded oratories, hospitals, and beautiful churches; they earnestly preached the Gospel; and they were the first to establish papal missions in foreign lands. Through

their work and good example, the Theatines encouraged priests and laypersons to lead holier lives. Four members have been canonized:

St. Cajetan (1480-1547) was born in Vicenza, Italy, studied law in Padua but decided to pursue a religious vocation, and was ordained at age thirty-six. In addition to founding the Theatine Order, he established a hospital in Venice for those suffering from incurable illness and founded a bank (which later became the Bank of Naples) to help the poor.

Bl. Paul Burali d'Arezzo (1511-1578) was born in Itri, Italy. A student of the future Pope Gregory XIII, he graduated from the University of Salerno and the University of Bologna. He served as a canon lawyer, a royal counselor to Emperor Charles V, and auditor-general of the army under Ferdinand of Toledo before joining the Theatines in 1557, and was ordained the following year. As a priest, he was appointed papal ambassador to the court of Spain for Pope Pius IV and superior of the Theatine houses of Naples and Rome. He was made a cardinal in 1570, implemented the decrees of the Council of Trent, and published a catechism for priests.

St. Andrew Avellino (1521-1608), a teacher of Lorenzo Scupoli, was born in Castronuovo, Sicily, became a doctor of civil and ecclesiastical law. In a courtroom argument on a friend's behalf, he committed perjury to support his position and was later so troubled by it that he gave up his practice of law for a life of penance. He joined the Theatines in his thirties and later as superior of the order he founded Theatine houses in Milan and Piacenza, Italy. His eloquent preaching, writing, and spiritual direction brought many people back to the Catholic Church.

St. Joseph Mary Tomasi (1649-1713) was born in Licata, Sicily, to a pious noble family; his parents later entered religious life, and four of his sisters became nuns. Joseph himself renounced his family's wealth to join the Theatine Order in 1665. He learned eight languages and wrote prolifically on theology, Scripture, patristics, and the liturgy. He enjoyed teaching children about the Faith and was noted for his knowledge, humility, and charity. ◆

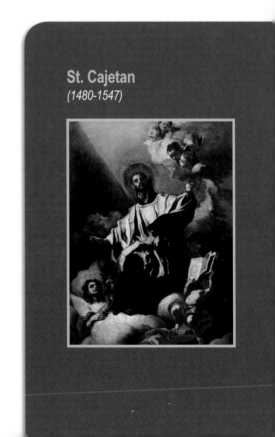

St. Cajetan
(1480-1547)

Sacramentals: Protection in the Spiritual Combat

Sacramentals are devotional actions and objects instituted by the Church to help us practice acts of virtue that obtain God's graces. These include the Sign of the Cross, blessings, certain devotions, holy water, and blessed objects, such as crucifixes, statues, medals, and scapulars. Sacramentals do not confer grace, as sacraments do, but they prepare us to receive grace.

Certain sacramentals are considered to offer spiritual protection. They are not magical charms, nor do they have power of themselves (though God's power can act through them), but they do help to turn our hearts toward God and remind us that He is our refuge and our hope Without His help, we are powerless against sin, the snares of the devil, and the lures of the world. Let's examine a few common sacramentals.

The Sign of the Cross
For centuries, Catholics have considered the Sign of the Cross to be a prayer of protection. St. Hippolytus, who died in the third century,

called the Sign of the Cross a protective breastplate of armor. In the fifth century, St. Peter Chrysologus said, "Let the cross be your helmet; let the cross on your forehead be your unfailing protection." St. Augustine and St. John Chrysostom also described the Sign of the Cross as a protection from the assaults of temptation and harm.

Since the persecutions of the early Church, Christians have made the Sign of the Cross in times of danger or fear as a prayer of protection. It expresses our belief that Christ has conquered darkness through the power of His love on the Cross.

Holy Water
Part of the Easter Vigil—the Mass celebrated the evening before Easter Sunday—is the blessing of water to be used for baptisms and other blessings. Traditionally this blessing of water includes a prayer of protection against evil and the addition of salt, a spiritual symbol of wisdom,

which pre-serves our faith. The holy water with which we bless ourselves on entering or leaving a church should also remind us of our baptism, through which we have become God's children.

The Brown Scapular

A scapular is a garment consisting of two small pieces of wool cloth joined by cords and worn over the shoulders. They come in various types, but probably the most common is the Brown Scapular, which the Blessed Mother presented in an apparition to Carmelite priest St. Simon Stock in 1251, with this promise: "Take this scapular; it shall be a sign of salvation, a protection in danger, and a pledge of peace. Whosoever dies wearing this scapular shall not suffer eternal fire." Wearing the Brown Scapular can remind us that Mary will intercede for us in our spiritual combat.

St. Benedict Medal

St. Benedict was the father of Western monasticism and was known not only for his Rule for holy living, but also for delivering people who were possessed by the devil. It is no wonder, then, that the medal of St. Benedict is an appropriate sacramental to assist us in the spiritual combat. The medal is rich in images that exhort us to be steadfast in our spiritual efforts. For instance, in the hand of the image of St. Benedict is his Rule, which reminds us that we must walk in God's ways, according to the Gospel.

Because St. Benedict is a patron of a happy death, the medal includes, in Latin, the inscription "May we be strengthened by his presence in the hour of our death." On the back of the medal is a cross bearing the initials of another Latin prayer: "May the holy Cross be my light! May the dragon [that is, the devil] never be my guide!" Circling the back of the medal are the initials of a Latin prayer of exorcism against the devil: "Begone, Satan! Never tempt me with your vanities! What you offer me is evil. Drink the poison yourself!" Those who wear this medal with devotion hope for St. Benedict's prayers and protection in their spiritual battles. ◆

A Treatise on Peace of Soul

Often included in editions of *The Spiritual Combat* is Dom Lorenzo Scupoli's brief *Treatise on Peace of Soul*. Although the latter title certainly sounds more tranquil than the former, achieving peace of soul requires struggle and perseverance, just as the spiritual combat does. In fact, Dom Scupoli makes it a priority: "The principal effort of our lives should be the quieting of our hearts, and the prudent guidance of those hearts, lest they go astray."

Throughout his treatise, Dom Scupoli emphasizes that our hearts must rest in God and that we must not be troubled by disturbances and worries that arise from sin, temptations, worldly cares, the actions of others, even religious devotions. Rather, we must focus on God and recall that He ordains everything we experience for our welfare.

We must not be disturbed by our falls, even if they are many, but must trust in God's mercy. Here is Dom Scupoli's method to follow after we have committed a fault: "Consider your own weakness, and humbly have recourse to God, saying to Him with a calm and loving confidence 'Thou hast seen, O my God, that I did what I could; Thou hast seen my impotence and, as Thou hast given me the grace to repent, I beseech Thee to add to my pardon the grace never to offend Thee again.' Once you have finished this prayer, do not torture yourself with anxious thoughts on your forgiveness, but without further adverting to your fall, proceed in your devotions with humility and ease, seeking the same tranquility and peace of mind as before."

This method will help preserve our humility and safeguard us against the devil's tendency to magnify our imperfections in our own eyes, which can alarm us and make it seem as if God has abandoned us. Humility will also protect us against another snare of the devil—the suggestion that we are superior to others—and lead us to look critically at their failings.

When our non-obligatory religious devotions become ends in themselves, rather than leading us to God, they themselves can disturb our peace of soul. Dom Scupoli urges us to be flexible in our devotions: "Strive not to limit yourself to so many prayers, meditations, or readings, neither neglect nor limit your customary devotions. Rather, let your heart be at liberty to stop where it finds its God, having no misgivings about unfinished exercises if He is pleased to communicate Himself to you in the midst of them . . . While God dwells with you, enjoy His company with the celestial peace of saints; and when His Divine Majesty pleases to retire, then turn again to the quest of your God in your devout exercises."

Sometimes God permits our peace of soul to be disturbed by thoughts and emotions that arise out of our self-love and natural inclinations. He does so for our own good. Likewise we might face spiritual dryness and find it hard to pray or to accept God's will. At such times, we must not become dejected or bitter or presume that God is angry with us. Rather Dom Scupoli tells us,

we must contemplate Jesus in His Agony in the Garden and imitate His prayer "Not my will but Thine be done." We must humble ourselves before God, persevere in our devotions, and try to retain peace in our soul through our acceptance of God's will.

With our hearts at peace, we will be better equipped for the spiritual combat. ◆

$Strong$ $Roots$

Dom Lorenzo Scupoli's Spiritual Influences

SCRIPTURE

2 Corinthians 10:3-4
"For though we live in the world we are not carrying on a worldly war, for the weapons of our warfare are not worldly but have divine power to destroy strongholds."

Philippians 4:13
"I can do all things in him who strengthens me."

Romans 7:22-25
"I delight in the law of God, in my inmost self, but I see in my members another law at war with the law of my mind and making me captive to the law of sin which dwells in my members. Wretched man that I am! Who will deliver me from this body of death? Thanks be to God, through Jesus Christ our Lord!"

Ephesians 6:10-12
"Be strong in the Lord and in the strength of his might. Put on the whole armor of God, that you may be able to stand against the wiles of the devil. For we are not contending against flesh and blood, but against the principalities, against the powers, against the world rulers of this present darkness, against the spiritual hosts of wickedness in the heavenly places."

Lorenzo Scupoli's wisdom, humility, and love for God have their origin in his spiritual formation: in the *strong roots of faith* that lie beneath the surface for every Catholic Classic. What were some of his strong roots?

Ascetical Theology

The spirituality of the Theatine Order, to which Dom Scupoli belonged, is an ascetical one. Asceticism, which comes from the Greek word *askesis*, meaning "training," refers to spiritual practices—prayer, self-denial, acts of charity, and so forth—that enable us to develop habits of virtue. Ascetical practices are meant to free the heart from sin, from worldly attachments and from self-love, so that it may respond to God in love and seek to please Him alone. Living an ascetical life as a Theatine enabled Dom Scupoli to offer in *The Spiritual Combat* so many practical ways to free our hearts to love God fully.

A Holy Novice-Master

Another Theatine, who himself wrote five volumes of ascetical works, had a particular influence on Dom Scupoli: St. Andrew Avellino, who received Dom Scupoli into the Theatine Order and was in charge of his novitiate. This deeply humble and pious priest was such an eloquent preacher and was so effective at converting sinners and heretics that his spiritual guidance was in great demand. Through St. Andrew's ministry and his example of holy living, his own disciple Dom Scupoli, in turn, would provide spiritual guidance to the multitude of readers of his *Spiritual Combat.* ◆

DID YOU KNOW?

The Spiritual Combat *was originally published in Venice in 1589 with twenty-four chapters. Subsequent editions contained thirty-three, thirty-seven, forty, and sixty-six chapters. The differing editions can support the view that the book is the work of a religious order, rather than of an individual writer, but it's likely that Dom Scupoli continued to work on the book after 1589 and contributed more chapters for later printings.*

"Fight the good fight of the faith; take hold of the eternal life to which you were called."

—1 Timothy 6:12

Christian Meditation

In *The Spiritual Combat,* Dom Scupoli recommends the spiritual practice of meditation as a way to deepen our love for God, overcome our vices, and cultivate virtue.

Many people associate the word "meditation" with Eastern religions which practice transcendental meditation. Although these practices are expressly forbidden in Scripture (Matthew 6:7), some have unfortunately found a place even among Christians. A person engaging in Eastern meditation seeks to liberate the soul from the domination of the body by emptying the mind (sometimes with the use of a mantra—a word or phrase repeated in order to eliminate conscious thought). Such meditation is believed to offer a wide range of benefits, from interior "enlightenment" and a higher state of consciousness to an enhanced immune system.

Regardless of such claims, transcendental meditation is not what Dom Scupoli advocates for the welfare of our soul and our eternal happiness. Christian meditation is a form of mental prayer in which, rather than emptying the mind, we engage it: we reflect upon Scripture or upon the life of Christ or the lives of the saints to discover ways in which we may grow in virtue and receive inspiration to do so. It's an essential aid to our spiritual combat because it deepens our knowledge of God, enables us to recognize our faults, and helps us to overcome them.

Aside from its preparation and conclusion, Christian meditation has three parts, which we can remember by using the acronym "CAR": considerations, affections, and resolutions. Let's consider each of these elements using as an example a meditation from *The Spiritual Combat* on Christ's Scourging at the Pillar and see how it can be applied to cultivating the virtue of patience.

Preparation: In his *Introduction to the Devout Life,* St. Francis de Sales recommends preparing for meditation by placing ourselves in God's presence and asking His assistance so that our prayer may be fruitful.

Considerations are points we think about concerning our topic. For our example, we would kindle a vivid image of Christ's scourging and reflect upon what Christ endured and how patiently He bore His suffering.

Our considerations should stir up *affections*, or good desires in our will, such as love of God and of our neighbor, spiritual zeal, compassion, thanksgiving, fear of judgment, hatred of sin, trust in God's mercy, and so forth. For our example, our considerations might arouse a desire to imitate Christ's patience during suffering and a greater love for the virtue itself.

Finally, these affections should move us to make *resolutions* to improve our lives. For instance, we might resolve, whenever we are tempted to react angrily to a person or a situation, to recall Christ's meek, gentle endurance of His scourging and to say a brief prayer asking for patience.

Conclusion: We conclude our meditation by thanking God for the affections and resolutions with which He inspired us, by offering Him our affections and resolutions, and by beseeching Him to grant us the grace to fulfill our resolutions. ◆

◆

"If, in uniting yourself to God, you become all His, and He all yours, what power or what enemy can ever harm you?"

—Dom Lorenzo Scupoli

Good Fruits

The Legacy of Dom Lorenzo Scupoli

The Spiritual Combat became a bestseller almost immediately after its initial publication in Venice in 1589. During its first twenty years in print, it was published sixty times and translated into German, Latin, French, English, and Spanish. Other editions, in Portuguese, Croatian, Polish, Armenian, Arabian, and Japanese followed. To date there have been as many as 600 editions of this Classic work, guiding innumerable Catholics, including saints, and even those of other faiths, to spiritual profit.

St. Francis de Sales
(1567-1622)

St. Francis de Sales, bishop of Geneva and Doctor of the Church, directed countless souls in his lifetime through his preaching, his teaching, and his letters. He continues to do so today through his published works—particularly his Classic, *Introduction to the Devout Life*. When his biographer asked him who his director was, St. Francis took from his pocket *The Spiritual Combat* and answered, "You see my Director in this book, which, from my earliest youth, has, with the help of God, taught me and been my master in spiritual matters and in the interior life. When I was a student at Padua, a Theatine Father instructed and gave me advice from it, and following its directions, all has been well with me." Later he would reveal that he carried the book in his pocket for eighteen years.

Bl. John Henry Newman

(1801-1890)

Bl. John Henry Newman, the illustrious clergyman, writer, and preacher who left the Anglican church to become a Catholic in 1845, was greatly influenced by *The Spiritual Combat.* As an Anglican priest examining Catholic spiritual works, he found in Dom Scupoli's book and in *The Spiritual Exercises of St. Ignatius* something that drew him into the Catholic Church: a living tradition and spiritual discipline that was much in accord with what he personally thought and taught. And not only did *The Spiritual Combat* help to lead Newman into the Catholic Church, it also continued to guide him as a Catholic and he often recommended it to others.

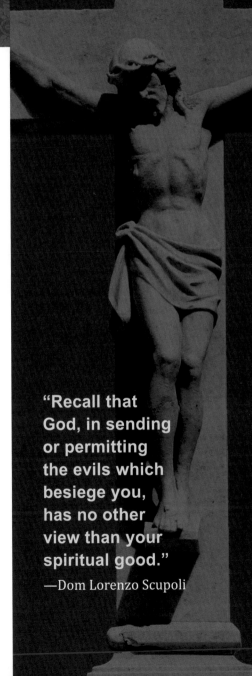

"Recall that God, in sending or permitting the evils which besiege you, has no other view than your spiritual good."

—Dom Lorenzo Scupoli

How to Read *The Spiritual Combat*

A Catholic Classic is not like other books. Properly read and meditated upon, it nourishes not only the mind but the soul: effecting in the reader an increase in *holiness* as well as knowledge. Follow this guide, based on the advice of St. Alphonsus Liguori, to get the maximum benefit from *The Spiritual Combat.*

First, set aside a quiet place and time. Novels and newspapers can be read on the bus or in a noisy house, but not a Catholic Classic. Pray before you begin, asking God to teach you the lessons he wants you to learn. Ask for Our Lady to be present, praying for and with you.

Have the right intentions. The purpose of spiritual reading is to grow in love of God and divine things, not to acquire facts, learn arguments, or indulge superficial curiosity. We shouldn't read a Classic just to say we have read it; we should read it because we want to be changed by it.

Read slowly and with attention. Like food that must be chewed carefully, spiritual reading requires some work in order to draw out its nutrients. Don't be afraid to linger over passages, prayerfully re-reading sections that confuse you or make a strong impression on you. Let's be like bees, says St. Alphonsus, who "do not pass from one flower to another until they have gathered all the nectar they found in the first."

Finally, come away from your reading time with some concrete intention **to take what you've learned and put it into practice**. Having received the spiritual wisdom of the saints, carry it with you in your heart, and put it to work in service of God and neighbor.

Spiritual Communion

My Jesus, I believe that You are in the Blessed Sacrament. I love You above all things, and I long for You in my soul. Since I cannot now receive You sacramentally, come at least spiritually into my heart. As though You have already come, I embrace You and unite myself entirely to You; never permit me to be separated from You. Amen.

O Lord, Who after creating me, did mercifully pay the price of my redemption, delivering me from the fury of myriad enemies, come now to my assistance; and forgetting my past ingratitude, bestow upon me this favor I now ask.

Behold, my God, Your creature, the work of Your hands, a man redeemed by Your precious blood. It is to You that I fly for aid, and it is in You that I place my entire confidence, for I know that You alone are infinitely good and powerful. Amen.

Putting It into Practice

The Spiritual Combat is full of practical ways to overcome your shortcomings and grow in holiness. Use this guide to help you put Dom Scupoli's advice into practice for a week, and see what a difference it makes.

Day 1: Trust in God

Below are just a few of the many Scripture verses that assure us that we will not be defeated if we trust in God. Reflect on one or more of these today and ask God to increase your confidence in Him.
— "The Lord . . . will not fail you or forsake you" (Deut. 31:8).
— "Those who seek the Lord lack no good thing" (Psalm 34:10).
— "Fear not, for I am with you; be not dismayed, for I am your God. I will strengthen you, I will help you" (Is. 41:10).
— "Let not your hearts be troubled, neither let them be afraid" (John 14:27).
— "I can do all things in him who strengthens me" (Phil. 4:13).
— "Cast all your anxieties on [God], for he cares about you" (1 Peter 5:7).

Day 2: Seek God's Will

Resolve to choose God's will over your own whenever you can. To motivate yourself to do so, Dom Scupoli recommends that you recall that God has set the example for you by loving and honoring you in countless ways, from creating you to redeeming you to guarding you continually. Call to mind today the many signs of God's love and providence in your life so that you may realize that only His will will bring you happiness.

Day 3: Combat Sloth

Sloth—spiritual laziness or apathy—is a dangerous obstacle in the way toward perfection. A good way to combat this vice is to fulfill your duties at the proper time and in the proper manner. Whatever commands you receive or tasks you must perform today, try to complete them at the proper time and with diligence.

Seven Days of Spiritual Combat

Day 4: Practice Patience

Dom Scupoli notes that we can't acquire certain virtues, such as patience, without practicing external acts of that virtue. Make an effort to speak with great charity and mildness to someone who tries your patience or who has injured you. If possible, perform an act of kindness for that person or help him in some way.

Day 5: Govern Your Words

Uncontrolled talking leads to many evils, whereas silence is helpful in the spiritual combat. Dom Scupoli explains that silence is usually accompanied by confidence in God, rather than in ourselves, and by a greater desire for prayer and facility in practicing virtue. Try to limit your speech today. When you must speak, follow Dom Scupoli's advice: "After you have decided what to say, eliminate some of it, because, in the end, you will always discover that you have said too much."

Day 6: Keep Your Peace of Heart

Peace of heart is essential to the spiritual combat. Dom Scupoli warns that a troubled heart is accompanied by self-love and that giving way to anxiety allows the enemy to strike us. Today, rather than worry about a problem or difficulty in your life, raise your heart to God and remember that every cross He sends you is for your ultimate happiness, even though you might not appreciate its value now. Then renew your trust that God will help you.

Day 7: Be Constant in Developing Virtue

Dom Scupoli tells us that we must make continual advancement on our journey to perfection, and therefore we should not avoid opportunities for acquiring virtue. Today, as an act of self-denial or to develop greater patience or charity, go out of your way to be kind to someone you find disagreeable, or when given a choice of tasks, complete the less-pleasant one.

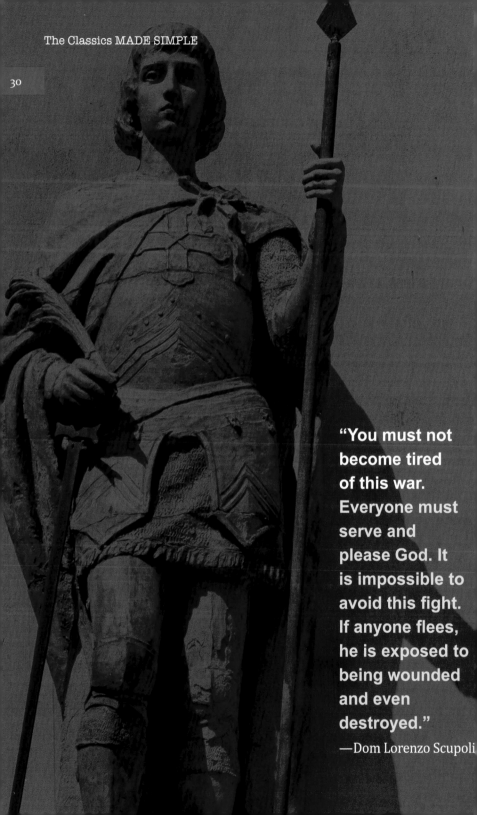

"You must not become tired of this war. Everyone must serve and please God. It is impossible to avoid this fight. If anyone flees, he is exposed to being wounded and even destroyed."

—Dom Lorenzo Scupoli

Words to Know

Calumny: The sin of lying in order to injure another person's good name.

Doctor: One of thirty-three officially recognized teachers in the history of the Catholic Church.

Lay brother: A non-ordained member of a religious order usually responsible for manual work and secular tasks.

Novitiate: The period of formal probation of a person in a religious order; during this time, the person is known as a novice.

Order: A community under a common religious rule.

Rule: A set of laws or regulations prescribed by the founder of a religious order for observance by its members.

Sacrament: An outward sign, instituted by Jesus Christ, by which grace and inward sanctification are communicated to the soul. The seven Sacraments of the Catholic Church are Baptism, Holy Communion, Confession, Confirmation, Matrimony, Holy Orders, and the Anointing of the Sick.

Self-denial: The act or practice of giving up some legitimate satisfaction for the sake of some higher motive.

Self-love: Inordinate regard for self to the neglect of others and indifference to their needs.

Spiritual dryness: In contemplative prayer, a period in which the heart seems separated from God, with no taste for thoughts, memories, and feelings, even spiritual ones.

Theatines: The Congregation of Clerks Regular of the Divine Providence, founded in Rome in 1524 to restore in the Church the primitive rule of apostolic life. Strictly austere, they were instrumental in advancing the Counter-Reformation.

Vice: The contrary of virtue, and, like virtue, a habit inherent in man and is the result of repeated sinful acts. A bad habit.

Virtue: A good habit that enables a person to act according to right reason, enlightened by faith, for the perfection of one's character.

Will of God: The manifest designs of God for a person's whole life or for any part of that life. The will of God can be known to some extent by the light of natural reason, through revelation, from the teachings of the Church, and through frequent prayer for divine guidance, daily reflection on one's moral conduct, and the counsel of a prudent adviser.

Additional Resources & Suggested Reading

Bauer, Benedict. *In Silence with God*. Scepter Publishers, 1997.

Chautard, Jean-Baptiste. *The Soul of the Apostolate*. TAN Books, 2008.

de Caussade, Dom Jean-Pierre. *Self-Abandonment to Divine Providence*. TAN Books, 2010.

Garrigou-Lagrange, Reginald. *The Three Conversions in the Spiritual Life*. TAN Books, 2002.

Newman, John Henry Cardinal. *Parochial and Plain Sermons*. Ignatius Press, 1997.

Robinson, Jonathan. *Spiritual Combat Revisited*. Ignatius Press, 2003.

St. Alphonsus Liguori. *Uniformity with God's Will*. TAN Books, 1982.

St. Francis de Sales. *Philothea or An Introduction to the Devout Life*. TAN Books, 2010.

St. Francis de Sales. *Thy Will Be Done: Letters to Persons in the World*. Sophia Institute Press, 1995.

Tanquerey, Adolphe. *The Spiritual Life: A Treatise on Ascetical and Mystical Theology*. TAN Books, 2001.